P

LIMEROONS

If you've never heard of a limeroon before, don't be surprised. You won't find the word in any dictionary. These humorous inventions are an original combination of limerick and cartoon and have been specially created for your delectation.

Immensely funny and highly entertaining, they feature all sorts of absurd creatures: a snake who is an adder and not a computer; a cuckoo who can't afford the rent on his own nest; a lion who ate the vet; a shark who has to be home before dark, and many more.

So give yourself a treat and dip into this mad menagerie of rhymes and nonsense.

Noel Ford is a full-time cartoonist whose work has appeared regularly in *Punch,* among other publications. *Nuts,* his first story for children, is published by Viking. He lives in Leicestershire.

LIMEROONS

Noel Ford

PUFFIN BOOKS

PUFFIN BOOKS

Published by the Penguin Group
Penguin Books Ltd, 27 Wrights Lane, London W8 5TZ, England
Viking Penguin, a division of Penguin Books USA Inc.
375 Hudson Street, New York, New York 10014, USA
Penguin Books Australia Ltd, Ringwood, Victoria, Australia
Penguin Books Canada Ltd, 2801 John Street, Markham, Ontario, Canada L3R 1B4
Penguin Books (NZ) Ltd, 182–190 Wairau Road, Auckland 10, New Zealand

Penguin Books Ltd, Registered Offices: Harmondsworth, Middlesex, England

First published 1991
1 3 5 7 9 10 8 6 4 2

Filmset in 13 on 16pt Monophoto Palatino

Printed in England by Clays Ltd, St Ives plc

'Please tell me,' the chimpanzee said,
'Is it true, what I've recently read?
Surely it cannot be
You're descended from me,
I thought monkeys were all so well bred.'

A polar bear grumbled, 'I wish
I had something new in my dish
Because, grill it or fry it
Or boil it, my diet
Is fish, fish, fish, fish, fish and fish!'

An ostrich, prim, proper and pert
Who buried her head in the dirt
Was mistook in the dark
For a tree in the park
And a passing dog gave her a squirt.

At the Animal Rescue I saw
A Rottweiler red-tooth-and-claw.
Did his owners desert him?
We'll never be certain.
He probably ate them both raw.

A chicken named Little once said,
'The sky's falling down on my head.'
A brainier bird
Might perhaps have referred
To our poor ozone layer instead.

As he slept on the old canyon floor,
A rock weighing two tonnes or more
Struck him clean on the shell,
But the tortoise just yelled,
'Go away, I'm not in, try next door.'

Do you think that one day pigs might fly?
And do fancy tricks up in the sky?
No! They're better at grunting
Than aerial stunting
And on the ground destined to sty.

In a frame of mind far from serene,
The chameleon said, 'It's quite obscene
The world's in a mess
And I feel so distressed.
I've a good mind to go and turn Green.'

A butcher I know called Joe Dawkin
Bought a parrot that wouldn't stop talkin'.
At the end of one week,
He held open its beak
And stuffed a large joint of best pork in.

A scholarly snake known as Fuchsia,
When asked by her elderly tutor
To divide six by nine
Replied, 'Teacher, please I'm
Just an adder and not a computer!'

I learned when attending night school,
Taxidermists have only one rule –
A creature must snuff it
And then you can stuff it.
(The other way round is quite cruel.)

When flying, the birds have it made.
It's rarely you'll see one dismayed
By strikes or by weather
For, frankly, they never
Have any of their flights delayed.

The chicken said, 'Doc I feel strange,'
But the doctor said, 'That we can change.
Though till you get over
Yer grave agoraphobia
You'll have to stop going free-range!'

A young scout named Benjamin Potts
Saw a snake attack two tiny tots.
In a nonchalant way,
Benji snatched it away
And then used it to practise his knots.

An elephant known as Selina
Was renowned for her helpful demeanour
But even she shrunk
From allowing her trunk
To be used as a vacuum cleaner.

At the rubbish dump, quite a commotion
Occurred when a bird voiced the notion
That a seagull's din-dins
Once came, not from slim tins,
But from some fabled place called the ocean.

A cow, now retired through ill health
Said, 'It's sad to be left on the shelf,
But that farmer's a punk,
All my milk that he's drunk
And never said, "Have one yourself"!'

A carrier pigeon once showed
How to carry a very big load.
As his wings madly beat
He rose two hundred feet,
But his leg still stretched down to the road.

Said a tired old tortoise named Bing,
'Hibernation is really *the* thing.
So, as I am dyin'
For a really long lie-in,
Don't wake me till quarter-past Spring.'

A cuckoo was heard to lament,
'My ways I have tried to repent.
I'd love to invest
In my very own nest,
But I just can't afford the darned rent.'

A dachshund named Wilhelm von Dent
Had a body remarkably bent.
His front end came hither
His back end went thither
As he tried to track down his own scent.

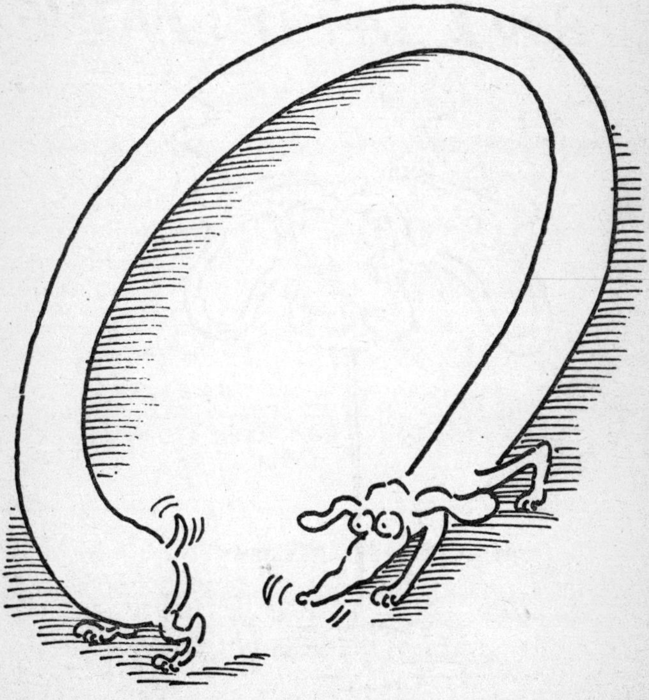

A flamingo I bought in a sale
Has only one leg, long and frail.
I've been told by the vet
If it breaks, not to fret.
There's a spare one tucked under its tail.

A glow-worm once asked a close friend,
'Have you got a crash-helmet to lend?
There's a well-meaning lout
Who keeps stamping me out
In mistake for a cigarette-end!'

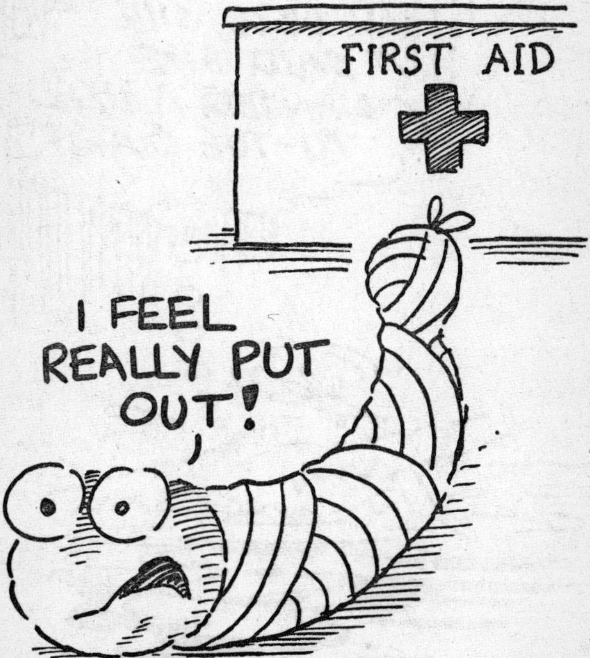

Wearing 'gater-skin shoes and tight breeches
She ignored the protesters' entreaties.
But she got quite a shock
When gulped down by a croc
Who said, 'Now who's an endangered species?!'

There once was a very sick lion
Who lay on his bed, softly cryin',
'My only regret
Is eating the vet
Before I found out I was dyin'.'

Against all her natural instinct
A sensitive skunk calmly drinked
A gallon or more
Of Chanel Number 4
And now, I'm afraid, she's ex-stinked.

The inch-worm appealed to the nation,
'Vote for me, it's your only salvation!'
But a young filly beat her,
Her name, Millie Metre
And that's how we got metrication.

Could you answer a small question, please?
Is it true that all mongrels have fleas?
Whilst the Kennel Club types
Have the best parasites
With impeccable family trees?

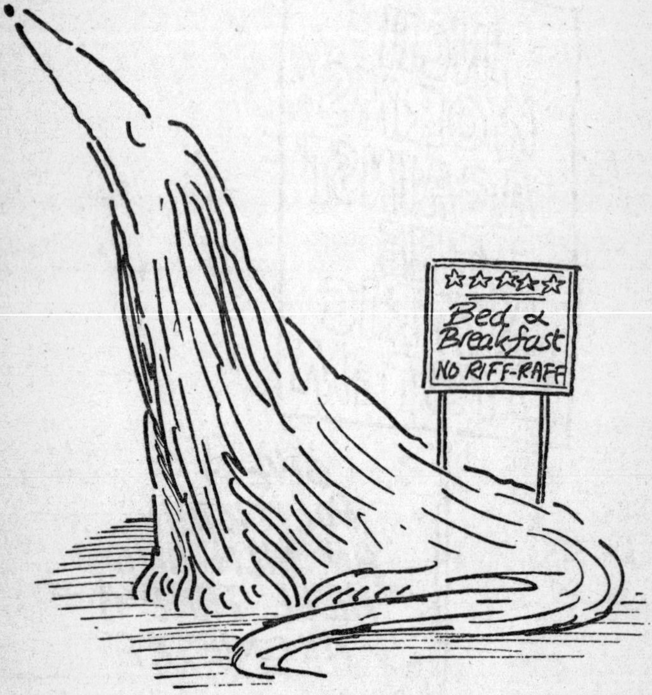

A kangaroo mum had a nipper
Whose favourite dish was a kipper.
But the pong from her pouch
Grew so strong, that she vouched
He must eat out or she'd fit a zipper.

The greyhound's remarkably fleet.
Well, let's face it, he hasn't much meat.
He might make a small stew
For an undersized shrew
But you'd still have to use all four feet.

A tortoise whose home was in Wales
Had his shell blown off in the March gales.
So he sold it complete
As a weekend retreat
To a couple of yuppy-type snails.

Let's hear a kind word for the shark.
Though his bite is much worse than his bark
He's not being rude
When he bolts down his food,
It's just mum wants him home before dark.

The most pitiful thing to behold
Is an elephant with a bad cold.
Even regular issues
Of double-strength tissues
Can't cope with what his nose can hold.

I've seen some incredible sights
Of creatures in various plights,
Like giraffes with their necks
Laid out flat on the decks,
Because they have no head for heights.

Stinging nettles are painful to some,
But not to the rhino, old chum.
When he sits down, those prickles
Are no more than tickles
To his armour-plate bullet-proof bum.

A promising artistic weasel
Had erected his miniature easel.
But his country lane scene
Turned out less than serene.
(He was squashed by a twenty-tonne diesel.)

A dinosaur expert, I quote
Said, 'This problem is getting my goat.
It seems very queer
They should all disappear
And not even leave me a note.'

If you're out shooting birds just for fun
Here's something to reflect upon:
Would you find it pleasant
To meet a large pheasant
If he was the one with the gun?

On Marathon Day, the whole street
Was closed to all traffic, 'That's neat!'
Said the hedgehog, 'I'll cross
While I cannot get squashed.'
And was flattened by ten thousand feet.

I've just heard it read on the news
That a pickpocket, ruined by booze
For kidnapping was nicked
'Cos the pocket he picked
At the zoo was a mum kangaroo's.

Young Caesar, a nectar collector
Heard a sneeze from the Queen's private sector.
'Oh the shame!' cried out Caesar,
'The Queen bee has hay fever
Workers rise up right now and eject her!'

A tortoise, remarkably slow
Ate ninety-six prunes in a row.
With an almighty shriek
He shot off like a streak,
Proving prunes can make anyone go.

A retriever named Tuppence one day
Was heard by her owner to say,
'I'm fed up with tricks.
If he wants those darned sticks,
Then why does he throw them away?'

There once was a stuttering sheep
Who'd repeat and repeat and repeat
B-b-b-b-b
B-b-b-b-b
B-b-b-b-b-b-b-BLEAT!

Brown bears, as you know, don't need money.
When they're hungry, they steal wild bees' honey
And, when stung on the tongue
They will shout, loud and long,
'I thuppothe you thig thagth very funny!'

A vampire bat friend of Count Dracula
Well-known for his use of vernacular
Lost his night-job in Sandwich,
Because constant bad language
Is something that bosses can sack-you-fer.

In New York, on a walk with our mother
A grizzly bear mugged my young brother.
But when asked to describe
His attacker, he sighed,
'Well, one grizzly is much like another.'

If you ever should meet such a creature
As the awfully fast-running cheetah,
You can run, if you like,
Or jump on your bike,
But the odds are he'll catch-yer and eat-yer.

The squid is a terrible fink.
He will squirt you before you can blink
And the only safe way
To approach him, they say,
Is to wait till he's run out of ink.

The octopus, as is well known
When busy will quite often moan,
'I've only four pair
Of hands, you're aware,
So you go and answer the phone!'

The elephant's trunk, like a hose,
Sucks up water wherever it flows.
But the beast must refrain
From drinking champagne,
As the bubbles go right up its nose.

The boa constrictor said, 'Please,
You don't need to feel any unease.
Don't do anything rash,
Just hand over your cash
And I won't have to put on the squeeze.'

Is it true, as the country-folk claim,
That cows always lie down before rain?
How can they be sure
That it's going to pour
With our weather forecasts?! It's insane!

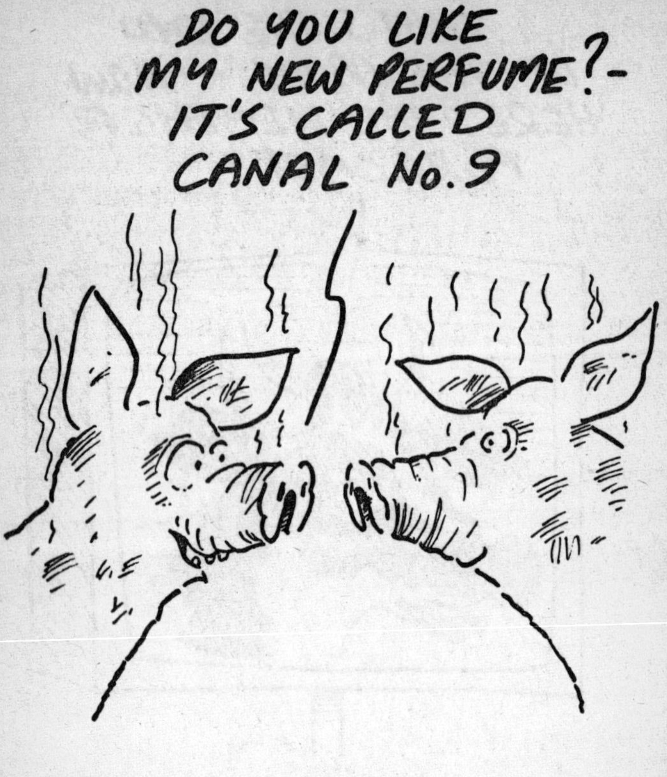

The stinkiest animal ever
Is the pig and, despite my endeavour
To find something smellier,
The nearest, I tell yer
Is a punk-band lead-singer named Trevor.

Now here is a tale, short but grim
Of a railway-mad rabbit, so dim
That he sat on the line
To catch the nine-nine
And the eight fifty-seven caught him.

The World Wildlife Fund man just frowned
Saying, 'Pandas don't often call round
With enquiries like yours
And we hate to be bores
But we simply can't lend you a pound.'

A black widow spider named Kate
Told her mother, 'I've found a new mate
And I can't help but wonder
If I've made a blunder
By eating him on our first date?'

As the year moved on slowly through June
The old caterpillar thought, soon
I must find bed and board,
But can I afford
To invest in a time-share cocoon?

The centipede said to the chimp,
'I know I'm a bit of a wimp,
But please cast an eye
As I walk slowly by
And tell me which leg has the limp.'

A platypus (duck-billed, of course)
With a voice of considerable force
On the stage set her heart
And soon landed a part
In the back of a pantomime horse.

As the butterfly spread her new wings
And flew round and round in wide rings
A young grub said, 'Gee!
You would never catch me
Going up there in one of those things!'

A fly on the ceiling said, 'Here
Aren't humans remarkably queer?
They walk round upside-down
High up there on the ground.
Oh, they're sure to come unstuck, I fear.'

Having measured the lanky giraffe
The tailor said, 'Don't make me laugh!
I would soon fall asleep
Counting all of the sheep
It would take just to knit you a scarf!'

As my husky-team started to sneeze
And tremble and shake at the knees,
I knew that I oughta
Put into their water
A little drop more antifreeze.

A knowledge of Indian skills
And a yen for unusual thrills
Led a sea-lion to buyin'
an' tryin' to lie in
A bed of best porcupine quills.

A TV-mad tortoise named Trish
For a satellite telly did wish,
So she stripped off – it's true!
And proceeded to view
With her shell as the aerial-dish.

Why's the hump on a camel's back found?
The answer is truly profound
If stuck on its tummy
It'd look very funny
And its legs wouldn't reach to the ground.

Said the Tit of variety Blue
To a bird of a similar hue,
'To be right up-to-date,
Set up home with your mate
In a satellite-dish made for two.'

As the lemming leapt into the sea
His technique was amazing to see,
But his quadruple spin
(With a back-flip thrown in)
Only scored him a poor five-point-three.

Some other Puffins

LIMERICK DELIGHT

chosen by E. O. Parrott

This marvellous medley of madness will spin you round and turn you upside down! Here are over 300 quirky and curious verses, olu favourites and new. Say them out loud, learn them by heart – dive in and have fun!

CROSSWORD CRACKERS

Colin Gumbrell

carefully thought out, original, and inventive collection of cross-ɔrds with clues covering a wide range of general knowledge.

MORE CROSSWORD CRACKERS

Colin Gumbrell

ıts may be easier to crack than these crosswords, but they aren't lf the fun! Three different sorts of crosswords ensure there's never lull moment with the puzzles in this fascinating and original book. ıether you're a beginner or an experienced puzzler, you can be tain that there will be plenty to intrigue and delight you.

PUZZLER'S A to Z

Colin Gumbrell

Puzzle your way from A to Z with these inventive and entertaining anagrams, word searches, shape and number puzzles, crosswords and quizzes of all kinds.

THE GREAT PUFFIN JOKE DIRECTORY

Brough Girling

Over 1,000 jokes presented alphabetically with Fat Puffin to guide you through. An original, hilarious book – you'll never be short of a laugh again!

CHUCKLE, CHUCKLE, THE CHILDREN'S JOKE BOOK

Ann Leadercramer and Rosalind Morris

An original and entertaining collection of jokes, puzzles and riddles from St Anthony's School Hampstead, in aid of the Wishing Well Appeal.

UP WITH SKOOL!

A book of jokes from children themselves, divided into ten sections including school dinners, homework and exams, and introduced by Mr Majeika.

THE SECOND PUFFIN CROSSWORD PUZZLE BOOK

Alan Cash

Another challenging crossword puzzle collection, including specialist puzzles for experts in science, literature and loads of other subjects. There are plenty of cryptic and general clues, too – enough to keep all crossword addicts happy.

THE PAIN-IN-THE-NECK JOKE BOOK

Martyn Forrester

The Pain-in-the-Neck Joke Book will keep you groaning from beginning to end. With vampire jokes, ghostly jokes, skeleton jokes, werewolf jokes, not to mention bat-ty jokes (geddit?) and monstrous jokes, you'll have a fantastic read. And who knows, maybe even *you* will be called a pain-in-the-neck when you've finished laughing.

A great book to suck up to your friends with!

THE HA-HA BONK BOOK

Janet and Allan Ahlberg

This joke book is full of old jokes to tell dads, mums, baby brothers, teachers and just about anybody else you can think of!